Rambling ROADS

CHARLES FILSON

ISBN 979-8-88832-230-7 (paperback)
ISBN 979-8-88832-231-4 (digital)

Christian Faith Publishing
832 Park Avenue
Meadville, PA 16335
www.christianfaithpublishing.com

Printed in the United States of America

Contents

One Life

Hold on to life as a precious jewel.
    Gold couldn't buy its worth.
The gift you were given couldn't be bought,
    With all the money on earth.

You have one life; don't give it away.
    Use it the best that you can.
Give to those worse off than you.
    Be a friend to man.

When time is done and you're standing there,
    Be happy with how you lived.
Think back on all you have accomplished.
    You have nothing more to give.

See Me

My mind shows me places I've never seen,
    Because I cannot see.
An accident took away my sight,
    But there's no bitterness in me.

Though I may no longer be able to see,
    I still have the other four.
I'm still able to be who I want to be,
    And stronger than before.

My eyes don't make me who I am.
    I've lost them, but I don't care.
It's who I am inside that matters.
    I have so much more to share.

You Were There

You changed my life since you entered it.
    I'm no longer a defeated man.
I no longer think of just myself.
    I give whenever I can.

I no longer have to go it alone.
    You're with me everywhere.
You showed me how to give of self.
    You showed me how to care.

Now as I come to the end of my journey,
    Free from heartache and strife,
I realize I was never really alone.
    You've been with me most of my life.

A Beautiful Day

I started the day off beautifully,
    Looked in the mirror (it cracked),
Tried to tie my shoes (they were loafers),
    Spoke to the walls—they spoke back.

Brushed my teeth with hair cream,
    Used toothpaste on my hair.
What I thought was deodorant was really room spray,
    So I smelled like the great open air.

Buttoned my shirt with one button left,
    Put on my pants inside out,
Put my shoes on—they were on the wrong feet.
    As you can tell, my day didn't work out.

There All Along

People have tried in so many ways
    To find some peace of mind.
They keep searching for it everywhere,
    But it's not so easy to find.

Peace of mind can truly be had
    If you let God take command.
He'll show you how to find peace in your life
    With a touch of the Master's hand.

People spend their entire lives
    Searching for a piece of heaven,
Never to realize the peace they seek
    Is in the life that they were given.

Changes

Due to reasons beyond their control,
    People are living on the street.
They're not any different than you or me.
    They're just trying to make ends meet.

They may not like the life they lead,
    So they refuse to become a part.
They search to find that inner peace
    That's buried in their heart.

They have the power to better their lives,
    To escape from misery and crime,
To become the person they were meant to be.
    All it takes is a matter of time.

This Stranger Became My Friend

There was a stranger, I am told,
    Who helped an old man carry his load.
The old man was too blind to see,
    So the load was given graciously.

The two men walked on silently,
    Then the old man spoke most earnestly.
He talked in length of days gone by.
    As he did, the young man began to cry.

Though troubles plagued the old man's life,
    He could feel a peace to end the strife.
For on the road to his journey's end,
    God sent a stranger to be a friend.

Going Home

I wished my brothers all good night
    Not knowing what lay ahead.
With morning only a few hours away,
    I climbed into my bed.

I dreamed of peace for all mankind
    And saw world hunger end.
I dreamt a dream of a righteous world
    And saw all people live as friends.

While fast asleep an angel came
    And woke me from my rest.
He told me God was calling me
    And I was going home at last.

Silent Communication

They don't use words we can understand.
    Their expressions are their voices.
They live without malice and know no fear
    In a world where they have no choices.

Their cries are silent, for few will listen
    To a world they can't understand.
For who will help the handicapped
    Or lend them a helping hand?

The cost is oh so very small;
    A kindly smile will do.
So please stop and listen to one who's in need.
    They might be calling to you.

Never Say Never

I know no limitations
On what can or can't be done.
If I feel it in my heart I can do it,
Then half the struggle is won.

I won't accept "can't" as an answer.
If it's impossible, I'll try.
I refuse to accept it 'til I try it myself.
Then I'll search for the reasons why.

If you search yourself for answers,
I'm sure you're going to find
The only limits a person has
Are the ones that are in his mind.

You Decide

You may not remember me, but I remember you.
    For the longest time we were friends.
I hoped you'd visit from time to time,
    But those hopes soon came to an end.

You turned your back and walked away,
    But I refused to let you go.
I watched your back never giving up hope.
    My love would eventually show.

I'll always be here to welcome you back,
    Whenever you decide to return.
But whether you believe or walk away
    Is a lesson you must learn.

The Reply

I'm surprised that you remembered me.
    We haven't spoken in years.
The things I said weren't very kind
    And would bring most people to tears.

Yes, I turned my back and walked away,
    But you loved me even then.
The names I called you I couldn't repeat,
    But you continued to call me friend.

I don't deserve the love you give
    After all I've done to you.
But you give it unconditionally
    After everything I tried to do.

Lonely Vigil

The rocking horse sits alone on the floor,
    Waiting for someone to play.
Silent and proud, he stands there erect,
    But no one is coming today.

The toys are all put away in the box;
    The models are stored on the shelf.
Still, the horse sits gently rocking,
    Left to play by itself.

Yes, the pony sits covered with dust,
    Waiting for someone to ride.
But no longer will he feel a child's weight.
    You see, the child has died.

Something's Missing

There was something missing in my life.
    Just what I couldn't tell.
Everything I ever did
    Would completely go to hell.

The simplest things I tried to do
    Completely slipped my grasp.
I know I needed the help of God,
    But I'd forgotten how to ask.

Now each night before I go to bed,
    I get on my knees and pray.
"Lord, if you hear me, walk with me,
    And give me another day."

Not Asking Much

In the beginning God created man
    And everything he'd need.
But man decided it wasn't enough,
    So he created greed.

Man wasn't contented with what God had done,
    So money became their god.
They didn't believe they made a mistake.
    They thought they were doing good.

God doesn't ask much, but He wants your love.
    And He'll show you where you've erred.
He asks so little, but He gives so much
    Because He's a god who cares.

Only Words

Words can surely wound the heart
    And cut as deeply as a knife.
They can easily tear a person down
    And ruin another's life.

Many people take great joy
    In hurting someone's pride.
They try to undo the goodness in others
    By wounding what's inside.

Though words have power to damage pride,
    You can lessen the harm that they do.
You can laugh them off or stand and fight.
    The choice is up to you

Not Written Yet

The future is the finish line.
How you get there is up to you.
Do you have what it takes to get to the end
And take pride in what you do?

Do you have the courage to see it through
And help others along the road?
Those who are struggling, too weak to go on,
Will you help them carry their load?

Your story hasn't been written yet,
But it'll take some time.
Yet at the end, people will know your name
When you cross the finish line.

Reminder

Most folks called him a homeless bum.
    His clothes were dirty rags.
The suitcases that he carried
    Were simple carpetbags.

He dressed this way to remind himself
    Of the life he used to live;
When he had nothing in his pockets,
    Even if he wanted to give.

Over time he gave away all he had,
    Which was quite a tidy sum.
He found more pleasure in the life he led
    When he was just a worthless bum.

Know Where to Look

True happiness isn't found in a bottle or can,
    Or in the pages of a book.
It can be found in the people around you
    Everywhere you look.

Look into the face of a child
    If it's true happiness you're after.
Watch people gather 'round the dinner table.
    See their friendship; hear their laughter.

True happiness can be found most anywhere
    If you open up your eyes.
If you've never experienced the thrill before,
    You're in for a big surprise.

Traditions

Traditions were created years ago,
     From generation to generation over time.
Each generation created their own,
     Then passed them to the next in line.

No one knows how they started,
     And each family has its own.
Nobody questions traditions.
     That's just the way it's always been done.

So start your own traditions,
     The kind you hope will last,
To be shared with the next generation,
     When your future becomes the past.

Role Reversal

Next time you're feeling a little too proud,
    That you're better than anyone else,
Think for a minute of those who have less,
    Then take a good look at yourself.

Have you ever thought how you would feel
    If you didn't have a cent,
Scraping together nickels and dimes,
    Trying to pay the rent?

Your book isn't finished; it's not too late.
    But you have to be willing to try.
If you don't change your ways and make amends,
    You could be the other guy.

Invitation

You're more than welcome to rest awhile.
    We don't need to know your name.
Makes no difference if you're black or white,
    Everyone is treated the same.

You're welcome to supper if you have a mind.
    Just find a place and sit down.
Don't be bashful; just pull up a chair.
    There's plenty of food to go around.

Stop again if you're ever by this way.
    You'll always find a smile.
We're friendly folk doing the Lord's work,
    So come and stay awhile.

Grudges

It's never easy to carry a grudge.
    They prevent you from getting ahead.
You're back starts to weaken, muscles ache.
    And another thing…they shed.

Grudges are wicked little creatures
    That do the bearer no good.
They will always hurt those that carry them,
    Who'd get rid of them if they could.

No one dares go near it.
    They fear the harm it will do.
Most folks see it and run away.
    Be careful, it doesn't cling to you.

Later

Make every day a memory
      That's worth remembering in days to come.
Be unafraid to make mistakes;
      March to a different drum.

Always be ready to lend a hand.
      Show someone you care.
Give comfort to those who need it most
      And try to always be there.

The rewards you receive are the smiles
      Of those you helped along the way.
The life you led while you were here
      Will be remembered on Judgment Day.

He Cares

"Angels, please watch over us
    And guard us as we sleep.
For tomorrow we have much to do
    And promises to keep.

"Please be with us through our waking hours.
    Help guide us through the day.
Be with us in the evening time
    As we get on our knees to pray."

Angels are a promise kept
    That God is watching from above.
They were sent to be His messengers
    To show us His true love.

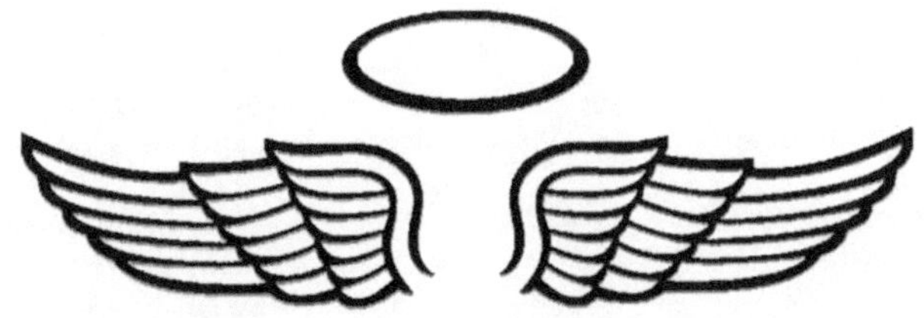

There All the Time

Kindness isn't something found in a book,
And it isn't taught in school.
But used correctly, you'll soon find
It will be your most valued tool.

All you need to do is open your heart.
The kindness you seek is there.
Be willing to give yourself a break
And show yourself you care.

What you're looking for is within you
That most anyone can see.
You've had it with you all along.
It just needs to be set free.

Earthly Magic

The world is full of magical things,
    If you only lend an ear.
The songbird singing in the trees
    Tells you God is near.

The brook as it slowly drifts along,
    Heading out to sea,
Says "Good morning" to the world,
    And how glad it feels being free.

Even in stillness the voice of God
    Can be heard among the trees.
He speaks to us in quiet tones
    And can be heard in a gentle breeze.

Answered Overnight

Each night before I go to bed,
    I thank the Lord on high
That He let me see another day
    And be always at my side.

I pray He guards those dear to me
    And those that I call friend.
Keep them safe away from harm
    And bring their troubles to an end.

I know my prayers are answered.
    His promises will always be kept.
I know because I trusted in Him.
    They were answered while I slept.

Am I Forgiven?

Good morning, God, it's me again.
    Thank You for another day.
Thank You for the sun that shines,
    But I must be on my way.

I don't have time to sit and chat
    Or even say a prayer.
With everything I have to do,
    Sometimes I forget You're even there.

It's evening now. I'm on my knees
    And praying now at last
That you'll let me see another day
    And forgive my offenses of the past.

I'll Carry On

As long as my legs will carry me
    And my heart beats in my chest,
I'll do what I can to help mankind
    Strive to do their best.

"The poor will be with us always," it's said.
    But if I can do my part
To ease their pain for another day,
    Then maybe they could make a new start.

My life was a gift, so why not give back?
    Maybe it'll start a trend.
If we all gave, it might light a spark
    And bring poverty to an end.

Go with It

Things will work out; they always do.
    Just relax and go with the flow.
Try to remember happier times.
    Sit back and enjoy the show.

Not everything is tailor-made
    To the way you think it should be.
You have to take things as they are.
    Just be open and carefree.

It's a give-and-take world we live in.
    Sometimes we give more than we get.
Though, with all of our imperfections,
    God's not finished with us yet.

The End

I was with you from the day of your birth.
    I watched you run and play.
I was with you as you aged and grew,
    And as you knelt to pray.

I'm with you through your waning years,
    And you haven't long to live.
I'm with you when you breathe your last,
    And you have nothing more to give.

Come home, my child. Your Father waits.
    Your race at last is run.
Sleep now beneath the ground you trod.
    Your days on earth are done.

Childhood Friend

I knew you many years ago
    When I was just a lad.
We played together many times.
    You were the closest friend I had.

We were always together, in sunshine and rain,
    Sharing sorrow and laughter.
My stuffed little friend, with button nose,
    Showed me the happiness I was after.

Now the years have gone; toys are put away.
    But whenever I need a friend,
My mind drifts back to my childhood days,
    And my loneliness comes to an end.

Too Much?

Many go to God with problems.
    That's what we were taught to do.
But how many people go on their knees
    With just a simple thank-you?

He said He'd answer our every prayer,
    So is it too much to ask,
Since He promised this to the least of us,
    Is saying thanks too big a task?

So next time you think of talking to God,
    Just try something new.
Don't just fall on your knees and pray for help.
    Make sure you thank Him too.

No Instructions

Life doesn't come with instructions
     Or a set of rules for living.
A brain and a heart to help you live
     Are the only tools you're given.

The heart may teach you how to live
     And help you to be strong,
But the brain will give you wisdom
     And teach you right from wrong.

But until the two work together,
     Common sense will have to step in
To try to end your confusion
     And help you start living again.

Think First

You don't need a lot of money,
        Fancy cars, or expensive yachts.
What you need is a life worth living
        To be happy with what you've got.

Just think of those with nothing,
        And you'll begin to realize
You're as rich as a king to those in need.
        And it's right before your eyes.

So before you start to grumble and moan
        About the money you never had,
Just keep in mind how things could have been,
        And you'll see things aren't that bad.

Individuals

Did you ever take notice of the people you meet,
    The girl in the subway, the man on the street,
The kid playing ball in the field with your son,
    Unaware that you've noticed their laughter and fun?

You may talk to them often, know them for years,
    But still you don't know their hopes and their fears.
Do you ever take time to give them a smile,
    To make them feel happy, even just for a while?

Take a second to listen,
    And I'm sure you will find
The person who's talking
    Is one of a kind.

Gotta Rush

Come relax and chat awhile.
    I haven't seen you in quite a spell.
Tell me now what's on your mind.
    I hope you're doing well.

You say you're busy; you can't slow down,
    Can't even say hello?
Life is too short for pleasantries?
    You really think you should go?

Maybe I'll see you again next time,
    And maybe you'll slow down.
We'll chat awhile and reminisce
    If you ever come around.

God's Gift on Loan

A child was born, a gift from heaven,
    In loving kindness was given.
An answered prayer sent from above
    To fill my loneliness with love.

An angel came the other day
    And took my child far away.
Now all I have is the memory
    Of just how much you meant to me.

So sleep in peace, dear little one.
    The night is gently falling.
Go to sleep and fear no more.
    I hear your Father calling.

An Understanding Friend

It's nice to know when things go wrong,
    There's someone to turn to amidst the storm.
Someone to tell your troubles to,
    I found that someone here in you.

A gentle word, a tender smile,
    Can ease the hurting for a while;
Can make the problems go away
    And give me strength to face the day.

Thank you for just being there.
    It shows me you're a friend who cares.
But more than that, I think it's good.
    It shows me you're a child of God.

No Bed of Roses

When troubles are upon you
	And your world begins to fall,
Just lift your heart in prayer to God.
	He's waiting for your call.

No eye has ever seen a rose
	That didn't have its thorns,
Nor seen a day that after rain
	The sun has never shown.

I've never faced a problem yet
	When I stood there on my own.
For God was always by my side,
	Our hearts were joined as one.

Utopia

Are you feeling down, depressed?
    Then come along and be my guest
Upon a magic carpet ride
    To a place where only peace resides.

This world of wild fantasy
    Will soon become reality
For unfulfilled dreams and hope unveiled
    And Cinderella fairy tales.

The cost is only just a smile
    To have your dreams filled for a while.
So put your troubles all aside,
    And come along and take a ride.

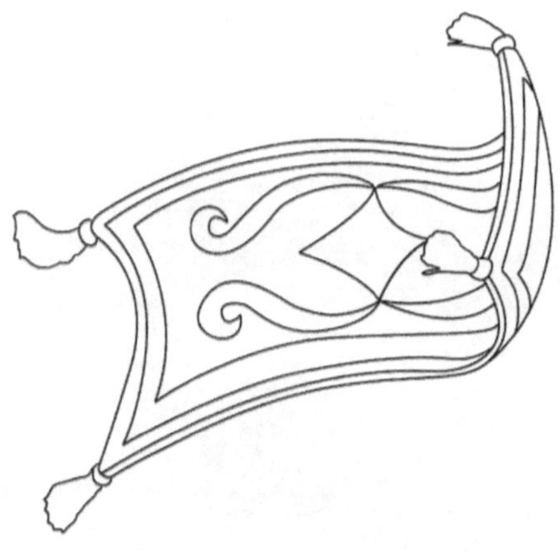

A True Friend

It isn't easy when you're sad,
       To face it on your own.
If you need a friend, just call my name
       And let me share your load.

I'm not like some, a babbling brook,
       Who will run to tell another.
I'll sit quietly and listen and keep to myself
       The problems which bring you sorrow.

I might not have the answers you seek,
       But of one thing I am certain;
My heart outstretched and always there
       To help you share your burden.

I Trust My Friend

Dear friend, I wish you many things
    Into your life may fall.
The blessings of joy and a tranquil heart
    That are offered to one and all.

May sorrow never darken your door,
    But love abide within.
May people live as you have lived
    And be a friend to man.

Whenever problems came to call,
    We weathered them together.
A truer friend I could not find.
    I would not ask for better.

P.S. I give to you my friend a gift
    To be guarded as well as you must.
This gift is more precious than gold itself.
    I give to you my trust.

I'm Going Home

On the morrow I am leaving.
    I shall not return again.
I go to meet my living God
    Aboard the Freedom Train.

Ahead lies endless riches,
    The likes I've never known.
On the shores of the Great Forever
    Is where I'll build my home.

When the roll is called up yonder
    And I stand before the Lord,
He shall see by my convictions,
    I lived his Holy Word.

I Can't Tell You, Lord

I: As I kneel here before you,
    My eyes turned toward the sun.
I thank you for your tenderness
    And the miracles you've done.

II: I thank you for your Son
    Who was sent to set me free.
But most of all I thank you, Lord,
    For watching over me.

Chorus:
I can't tell you how much, Lord,
    You've changed my life.
And every time I let You down,
    You brought me through my strife.

III: If thanks could only say, my Lord,
    All that's in my heart,
Then thank you, Lord, for loving me.
    We'll never be apart.

A Prayer for the Children

God, grant children everywhere
    A life of joy and free from care,
A world of hope so they might be
    No burden to humanity.

In times of sorrow, give them peace
    And keep them safe from harm.
Comfort them in times of strife
    Under your protective arm.

In a world where children have no voice,
    You are their only hope.
So help them grow to understand
    So each may learn to cope.

How Do You See Me?

And I, too much "I," and not enough "We,"
　　Only concerned with what concerns me?
Do I get angry if things don't go as planned?
　　Am I eager to help my fellow man?

Am I ready to practice what I preach,
　　Willing to learn what others might teach?
Do I learn a lesson from my mistakes,
　　Able to give much more than I take?

If called upon, am I eager to serve,
　　Ready to praise what I know is deserved?
If I can answer yes to the above,
　　Then I'm on my way to understanding love.

About the Author

Charles was born in 1953, the third of seven sons. He was born with cerebral palsy and seizures. He started writing when he was in high school, but he started writing seriously after graduating in 1971. That's when he started volunteering with an organization to help handicapped individuals. He started writing about their trials and how they overcame them. In 1987 he became a Special Olympics bowling coach.

He lives in Lansdale, Pennsylvania.